ITY NOW! SERIOU

T! WHAT THE?!? HEY ... T DA

AT? GASP! AHHH! GEE WHI

H MY GOODNESS! WHAT IS THAT? GASP!

UMANITY! SERIOUSLY??? THERE'S NO W

! WHY OH WHY? SERENITY NOW! OH THE

DARN IT! WHAT THE?!? HEY! WHY OH WH

HAT IS THAT? GASP! AHHH! GEE WHIZ! S

?? THERE'S NO WAY! OH MY GOODNESS! W

NITY NOW! OH THE HUMANITY! THERE'S

ARN IT! WHAT THE?!? HEY! WHY OH WHY

SLY??? GASP! AHHH! GEE WHIZ! SHOOT

Y! OH MY GOODNESS! WHAT IS THAT? GA

ITY NOW! OH THE HUMANITY! THERE'S N

THE?!? HEY! WHY OH WHY? SERE

ASP! AHHH! GEE WH

CONTENTS ARE EDUCATIONAL & TRUE

WARNING

YET BIOLOGICALLY GRAPHIC

DISCLAIMER

The book in your hands was not written by a doctor, a scientist, a professor, or an expert of any kind; the author is simply a dad. The facts in this book have been researched and sources have been cited however, the author asks that you investigate further before making any decisions or forming concrete opinions based on information found in this book. The contents should be considered the author's opinions based on real facts. The author is not responsible for any harm caused by misinformation acquired before, during or after reading *40 Shocking Facts For 40 Weeks of Pregnancy.*

40shockingfacts.com
Twitter: @joshuabest

Printed in the United States of America

Ingram Printing & Distribution, 2015

ISBN-10:0-9861931-0-0
ISBN-13:978-0-9861931-0-1

Unprecedented Press LLC
1336 Logan St. SE
Grand Rapids, MI
49506

Twitter: @UnprecdntdPress

Photos by Kyle Bultman Photography

First Edition

Unprecedented
Press

40 SHOCKING FACTS
FOR 40 WEEKS OF PREGNANCY

Joshua Best

Volume 1:
DISTURBING DETAILS ABOUT
CHILDBEARING & BIRTH

For my wife and editor, April.
Thanks for pushing.

TABLE OF CONTENTS

☞ BIRTH ☜

INTRODUCTION

I'm not qualified to write a book about babies. I'm not a pediatrician, a midwife, a specialist, a psychologist, or anything that ends in "ist". Truly, I am not qualified to write this book. The truth is, I'm just a guy, just a guy who became a Dad.

When it comes to experience, and education, the *only* relevant title I hold is "Dad." It's my only credential. In fact, it's the only thing that allows me to even *discuss* the topic of having kids. It begs the question – does that give me enough clout to write a book about having kids? Possibly not. On the other hand, the title doesn't exactly imply gravitas. I do, however, think that my lack of experience gives me a unique perspective, the perspective of a regular guy. There aren't many books written by regular guys because tradition tells us their opinion doesn't matter. For that reason alone, I knew I needed to write this book.

The baby industry is dominated by experts, psychologists, and doctors of many kinds. Every writer in the field has an opinion that is grounded in their years of training. In theory, those are the people we should be listening to. That being said, how is the average person with no baby knowledge whatsoever supposed to catch up to the level of their professional discourse in just nine months? It's impossible.

When my wife became pregnant with our first child,

I noticed she was starting to read baby books, and lots of them. One day, she approached me, and said, "Unless you do some research, I refuse to make baby-related decisions with you. Here's what will happen: I'll be informed, and you'll be uniformed, but you'll still demand an equal say in every choice. I need you to read at least one book."

She made a good point, and it's true – I tend to form opinions about things I don't know much about. It's a dangerous habit, so without haste, I found a baby book and started reading. After I finished it, I took a couples' class with my wife which was administrated by hospital. They showed us how to breathe during labor, how to swaddle a baby, and what we should expect at the hospital.

After giving birth to our baby boy, I realized that most of parenthood exists in a bubble. Unless you're a parent (and have taken these classes), you have no idea what goes on in baby world. There is some seriously gruesome stuff! I always knew I wasn't an expert, but I had no idea that I was so sheltered from the shocking details.

Perhaps, it's a man thing. A lot of this is related to women's health, after all. Men aren't granted access to that world. Unless you attend all of their doctor appointments, when would you ever hear this stuff? Perhaps, it's an age thing. Teenagers are taught the basics in health class and by their parents at home, but who wants to teach their kids about breastfeeding or exercising your vaginal floor? It would be *so* awkward. My mom was a nurse in labor and delivery, and I *still* had no clue. In her defense, I have three brothers and zero sisters, so I can see how approaching the topic would have been tough.

When I was in my early twenties, I would purposely leave the room if anyone was talking about childbirth. I simply didn't want to know. I wanted to remain ignorant. Looking back, I still understand that point of view. Why would you want to immerse yourself in a strange world if you don't have to? In fact, if I could have remained oblivious for a few more years, I think I would have. I mean, you wouldn't tour nursing homes at age forty, so why learn about babies at twenty? My point is – I was in the dark.

I don't think experts realize just how much of what they discuss is new information to new parents. For me, reading my baby book was like reading a martian language. They've been studying this topic for so long that they drop information bombs like they're common knowledge. When we finished our first baby class, I looked around the room, and half of us were left with our jaws hanging open after the first thing they said.

The shocking facts about childbirth deserve a bit more "tadaa!" They deserve to be treated as new information, because for many new parents that's what they are. This book is an attempt to present the most shocking things I learned in the way I would present them to a friend: as shocking. I don't presume this will serve as a full guide to the experience of having a baby, but maybe it will help new parents catch up on the discussion a bit quicker. This is a book for people who don't want to be caught unaware like I was. Hopefully, when someone mentions one of these shocking facts down the road, you don't have to pretend you already know, when deep inside you're actually freaking out.

There are 40 shocking facts in this book: one for each week of pregnancy. Read one a week, and with any luck, you'll be a bit more prepared for your big day. Or if you like, you can approach this book like a band aid, and just rip it off all at once. Good luck!

SHOCKING FACT #1
THEY'RE LISTENING

I'll be the first one to say that the order in which babies' features and functions develop makes absolutely no sense. At least not to me. I'm sure God gets it, and I hope there are a handful of doctors that understand what's going on in there, but from a new dad's perspective, it's very odd. On one hand, it takes years to develop knee caps. On the other hand, a baby is able to hear sounds after just twenty weeks in the womb. That's right – even before a baby is born, they're able to hear. Even before they have a birth certificate, or a name, before they're held for the first time, and before they achieve any other rite of passage into the world, they're able to hear.

You might be thinking about how amazing that is, and how beautiful the human body can be, but before you go too far down that road, let me propose an alternate train of thought. Many people think that speaking to their baby early on is super special. I don't disagree, but in a sense, it's a little creepy. Think about it. The NSA gets a ton of backlash for listening to our conversations, but somehow at just twenty weeks in the womb, our babies get to hear every little thing we say. Maybe that's not creepy; maybe it *is* actually magical. The fact they can identify your voice when they're born *is* pretty amazing.

Whatever you do, don't forget – when you're half way through your pregnancy, and you're having that conversation where you blame your significant other for not using birth control – your kid can hear you. If that doesn't make you think twice about what you say, I don't know what will. You didn't ask for my advice, but here it is anyways: always speak positively about your kids, and start it early. You may not have planned things to go this way, but children are always a blessing.

SHOCKING FACT #2
AT NIGHT,
THE TABLES TURN

Women have it rough. *They* grow the baby, *they* gain the weight, *they* get the morning sickness, *they* push the baby out through their genitals, and *their* body feeds the little tike. And that's just a snapshot! When will men have something to put up with? The gender tally chart is extremely lop-sided.

I can't say this fact is the great equalizer, or something that restores the balance of pain endured by each partner, but perhaps it can help. According to research, it's quite common for pregnant women to start snoring. It's caused by a combination of weight gain and the active hormones which enlarge mucus membranes resulting in nasal congestion.

After years of men having the market sewn up on snoring, the tables have finally turned. The refreshing news here is not that pregnant women snore (indeed, snoring isn't something you ever want to do), it's that men finally have something they need to endure.

The victim of snoring is rarely the snorer (although it could be a result of another medical condition, so if it's serious, see a doctor). No, the primary victim is typically the significant other, the one who is laying beside the snorer, unable to sleep, staring at the ceiling for hours on end, clenching their pillow, and planning to use it as a weapon. It won't make up for the pain endured by a woman giving birth, but it's nice to have just a little poetic justice.

SHOCKING FACT #3
KEGELS ARE NOT LIKE SQUATS OR CURLS

I remember it clearly; our birth instructor was teaching the ladies in our class how to exercise while being pregnant. I had seen them with that big, inflatable ball on TV, and thought that was perfectly normal. One exercise being taught was called Kegels. I hadn't heard of the name, but it sounded similar to "squats" or "curls," so I thought nothing of it. After all, a little exercise never hurt anyone.

As it turns out, Kegels are not just any exercise.

They're not just any pregnancy exercise either. According to doctors, Kegels are an exercise that can strengthen the muscles in the vaginal floor, which form a figure eight around the vagina and anus. Needless to say, it's wise to have those muscles at their best, and in peak physical condition by the time contractions hit.

So there I am with eight other couples, looking around the room, hoping not to catch anyone's eye, as we learn about Kegels (essentially push-ups for the vagina). It was shocking, but not awkward yet. It only became awkward when it came time to practice. The instructor said, "Go!" and no one moved. It's the only exercise that you can't actually witness anyone doing. It didn't help the situation when she told the men that we should join our wives in doing the exercise for the sake of solidarity.

What do you do in a moment like that? All you can do is hope you never see any of your classmates ever again.

SHOCKING FACT #4
BOOBS GROW

I am a man. If you are not a man, you may not relate to the emotion in my voice when I explain this shocking fact. Or maybe you will. Either way — I'm going to ask you to remember that I am a man who just can't help it. Here we go.

I like boobs. There I said it — I like them. And if you didn't already know, let me be the bearer of great news. During pregnancy, women's breasts get larger. Can you hear the angels singing? It's simply wonderful! If you didn't know it already, I'm honored to have brought a ray of sunshine into your day. If you did know (and I assume most of you did), let's all just take a moment to celebrate together.

Okay, that's enough celebration. Let's get back to reality. In the real world, this blessing doesn't really deliver on the benefits advertised. In fact, the aforementioned breasts are typically too tender to even touch. For me, it was like being the security guard who watches over the Mona Lisa. It's a masterpiece and a pinnacle of beauty, but there's not a chance in the world you'll get to touch. You'll see them everyday, but only from afar. In a sense, you're responsible for their new found glory, but at this point, the best thing you can do is keep your distance, and enjoy the view. So, put away your party hat, and keep your hands in your pockets.

If you're a woman, prepare yourself for being sore. Always and everywhere. Is this Mother Nature's cruel joke? Maybe, I don't know. But *this* I do know

– in all the world, there's not a more accurate definition of the word *bittersweet*.

SHOCKING FACT #5
NIPPLES GROW

See previous chapter, and replace each instance of the word *boobs* or *breasts* with *nipples*.

SHOCKING FACT #6
PREGNANCY BRAIN IS REAL

I'm sure most of you have heard of pregnancy brain. It has other names like momnesia, or baby brain farts. Okay, that last one's not real. I made it up, but don't worry – it's all in the spirit of an underlying point. If you haven't heard of this phenomenon, let me recap briefly. Pregnancy brain (these are all colloquial terms) occurs when a woman has a mental lapse in memory or focus, which is then attributed directly to being pregnant. The implication is that there is a chemical or biological shift that happens when you become pregnant which sabbotages brain function in relation to daily tasks. Like I said, I'm sure that most of you have heard of this, so this shocking fact is not about the existence of the belief itself, but the existence of facts which prove the belief.

Imagine for a moment that when you wake up tomorrow morning, you walk down the street, you pass the newstand, and on the cover of the New York Times you see this headline, "Bigfoot is Real!" It would grab your attention, right? Don't for a second pretend that it wouldn't; it would. That situation – though exaggerated – is comparable to this one. For centuries, men have been afraid to mention pregnancy brain, hoping it was a glitch in the matrix. Women, on the other hand, have been playing the pregnancy brain card for ages, using it to explain any type of slip up, large or small. Well, forget all of that; it's in the past. This is our new reality: scientists can support the existence of pregnancy brain.

Before you get too wound up, let me say that it's not a specific ailment that can be diagnosed. Instead, it's simply a result of the effects of pregnancy on a woman's mind and body, and if you think about it, some of these things are pretty obvious. Researchers say that a lack of sleep has significant impacts on memory retention, and it's common for pregnancy to keep you up at night. Also, the surge in hormones that rushes through a woman's body throughout pregnancy and labor can affect brain circuits. Plus, a pregnant person's priorities shift. They tend to focus on the very scary, life-altering event before them, as their bellies grow right before their eyes. According to experts, people can only truly focus on a few things at a time, and if a large portion of thought and mental capacity is given to preparing, or stressing about motherhood, it's likely that other everyday tasks won't get the same attention.

If you thought this chapter was going to be a big announcement of a scientific discovery, I'm sorry to let you down. There's no big press release here, just a handful of obvious realizations. My only suggestion for you is this: convert your disappointment into sympathy for the closest pregnant person you can find. Their forgetfulness is not a conspiracy, an excuse, a disease, or a myth. They're probably just stressed out, and really, really tired.

SHOCKING FACT #7
THERE ARE RULES FOR SLEEPING

I n my opinion, pregnancy favors the organized person. If you're someone who is put together, you check all the boxes, and you can keep things straight, you'll probably do pretty well. However, if you're not detail-oriented, and you can't keep things in order, you may have a tough time. There are so many i's to dot and t's to cross when it comes to pregnancy. The amount of reading you can do on the topic is endless, the amount of research and study is infinite, and the conversation about the best methods for this or that goes on and on and on.

If you're able to keep these things straight, and it comes naturally, I don't think you should be concerned. It's the rest of you I feel for – the ones who don't like to read, do research, or think about anything too far in advance.

The checklist has become so long that it now includes guidelines on how to sleep. Yes, they even have an opinion on how pregnant women behave when they're unconscious. As obvious as it seems, the first rule is that you're not allowed to sleep on your belly. If you can't guess why, then I'm not sure you should bring a child into the world. You'd better hope they turn out smarter than you are.

The second commonly published rule came as a surprise to me. Not only can you not sleep on your belly, but it turns out you shouldn't sleep on your back either. When a pregnant woman sleeps on her back, it restricts the flow of blood returning to the heart. In turn, that restricts the supply of blood to the baby, meaning they may not be getting as much oxygen or as many nutrients as they need. So what does that leave you with? If you're pregnant, it pretty much leaves you with the sides – left or right. Oh, but wait! Some sources also say your right side is a no-no for the same reason you shouldn't sleep on your back. In fairness, the harm of sleeping on your right side is disputed, but come on! As if pregnant women don't have enough to worry about. Now they have to get everything correct, even while they're asleep! I'd say sweet dreams, but I don't really see that happening, so I'll just wish you good luck.

SHOCKING FACT #8
IT'S ALL IN
THE BACK NINE

One of the reasons I wrote this book is because I knew there was a market for it. That's right—you've been had. But seriously, when people have babies they really want to buy stuff. It's a fact of life. Call it nesting, call it due diligence. Whatever you call it, you can't deny that the baby industry is huge.

Nowadays, it's not all books and bottles in the baby aisle. No—there are apps now. Lots and lots of apps. The moment we discovered my wife was pregnant, she downloaded a pregnancy app that tracked not only her progress, but the baby's progress too. I don't know why it's important to know what fruit my baby is closest to in size, or why they thought that wasn't offensive. I did, however, discover how heavy the baby was at any given time.

A couple weeks into her third trimester, my wife pointed out that our baby was the size of a grapefruit and weighed only three and a half pounds. Without thinking it through, I said, "that's awesome!" Then it hit me. "Wait — our kid is going to be tiny!" When I did the math, it didn't add up. We were more than two thirds through the pregnancy, but she weighed only half the normal weight. At this rate, she would weigh just 5.25 pounds at birth!

I'm grateful for my wife. She does most things better than I do, including preparing for a child. She politely informed me that babies gain most of their weight at the end of pregnancy. In fact, it's an amazing acceleration that takes place. Babies gain approximately fifty percent of their birth weight during the final nine weeks in the womb. In the final month, they can grow half a pound per week!

At any other time in life, that rate of accelerated weight gain would be alarming. Family members would be concerned. Friends would be staging interventions. Doctors would be recommending lifestyle changes. But no, not in the womb. The womb is an entirely unique ecosystem with a separate set of rules. The laws of nature as we know them don't apply there. In the womb, a human being is formed in just 40 weeks. In the womb, God shows off.

SHOCKING FACT #9
THE TRUTH WILL SET YOU FREE

When teaching new parents about the challenges ahead of them, there's no need to embellish; fact is stranger than fiction. The stark realities of pregnancy and childbirth are outlandish enough to serve as their own folklore. In my opinion, there are two aspects of the experience that really lend themselves to tall tales: gender guessing and encouraging the arrival of an overdue baby.

I can attest to both of these, but I'd like to focus on the second topic. When my wife was pregnant with our first munchkin, she was overdue by one week. I remember packing our emergency baby bag three weeks before the due date, and because I was ready practically, I was also ready mentally. After forty weeks of sharing her body with another person, she was anxious for it to be over, so we were poised for action three weeks early.

If you have access to the internet, you have access to a gold mine of tips on how to speed along an overdue baby. You'll find every type of home remedy from cleaning the house to drinking castor oil. Some of these are more legitimately proven methods, but others are simply old wives' tales. Some couples are so desperate to get on with it, they engage in superstition if there's even a slight chance it will work. My personal favorite of these home remedies is having sex. That's right, there is some evidence that having sex when overdue can help induce labor.

Pregnancy changes the hormone balance in women significantly, so it almost always causes changes in their libido. I've heard of some couples whose sex life improves in the second trimester, but I think the more common change occurs in the third trimester, when it becomes awkward just trying to have sex. The woman's comfort level drops significantly in the last couple months of pregnancy, so sex becomes more difficult, and may happen less often. That's why the suggestion to have sex to induce labor is a godsend for us men. We won't be having sex for sometime after the baby comes, and we may not have had sex at all in the last weeks or months because of her discomfort, so this old wives' tale becomes our best friend. In fact, I'm convinced there is a male-led conspiracy to perpetuate this belief. I can picture men anonymously dropping hints on baby websites and mommy blogs, suggesting sex as the remedy for all types of ailments. I'm convinced that this old wives' tale isn't an old wives' tale at all; it's an old husbands' tale.

SHOCKING FACT #10
IT'S MORE THAN AN ACRONYM

When I was a kid, my mother used to buy juice in a can. Not a typical pop can, but a can of frozen orange juice concentrate. I loved being the one to pop the aluminum top off, dump that frozen cylinder of condensed nectar into a big jug, add the four extra cans of water, and try to pummel the frozen chunks that were swirling the jug into oblivion. I remember being amazed that such a little can could provide my whole family with orange juice for a week. There's just so much stuff packed into that small space. Recently, I relived the same feeling of amazement when I discovered what a VBAC was.

When I first heard the term, I thought it sounded like a science fiction term, or maybe a robotics company, or a special, new high-tech lithium battery. Boy, was I wrong! The term VBAC is actually a medical term that stands for Vaginal Birth After Cesarean. If you didn't see that coming, I apologize. We'll get through this. I promise. Just hang in there.

I don't think I've ever come across an acronym that packs such a serious punch! Let's try to analyze why this term is so jarring. For starters, each of the four letters stands for a larger word, so in terms of length, the term is concentrated. Secondly, each word in the acronym carries its own meaning, which also adds to its depth. Third, the words that these letters represent aren't normal, everyday words used in conversation. For instance, you would never use the word "vagina" or "Cesarean" in small talk with your accountant. (If you do, seek help). Embedded in three out of four of these words is an inherently taboo association. This term just keeps expanding!

The fourth, final and most significant reason this itty-bitty acronym carries so much umph is because it exposes the person learning its meaning to some extremely personal info about the teacher. Simply by using the term, there's an implication that it's relevant to you, so you end up sharing personal information about your past and future. The implication is that she (or you, if you're a woman) needed a C-section last time she (or you) gave birth. It also implies she doesn't (or you don't) want another one. They say it's difficult to give birth vaginally after having a C-section, and not all hospitals allow you to even try.

One fine day, my wife's friend used the term, and I asked what it meant. I didn't know that I was *actually* asking her how everything went last time she gave birth (hence the "after Cesarean"). I was also asking her about her hopes for the next time she goes into labor. I wish I could warn men to look the term up instead of asking what it means when you hear it for the first time. At least, if you're reading this book, and you didn't know what it meant, now you do. I have single-handedly spared you some pain. You're welcome.

SHOCKING FACT #11
WATER DOESN'T BREAK ON CUE

If you've ever seen a movie with a pregnant woman, you probably know when labor starts. It usually goes something like this. The pregnant woman is giving a board room presentation or a speech in front of a large crowd (for maximum comedic effect), when all of a sudden — splash! The woman and two or three nearby victims are drenched in water. Cue laugh track. Cue labor.

That's what we know from show business about going into labor. Unfortunately, it's light years away from the truth. As far as I'm concerned, it's science fiction. The truth is far less funny and far less predictable. Most times, the water doesn't break like that. It's not an almighty sign from the universe that labor is starting. Nope. In fact, only fifteen percent of labors start with the water breaking. Most just start with contractions, and the water breaks sometime later in the process.

Let's recap. If a woman's water breaks, is she in labor? Yes. Does it mean she hasn't been in labor for some time? No. Is it still going to be gross and awkward? Absolutely.

So, if a woman's water ever breaks near you or on you, don't announce to the world that labor has commenced. Chances are she's been in labor for some time, and now you've exposed yourself as a clueless dimwit, as you simply state the obvious.

AN EPIDURAL IS NOT A PILL

Don't ask me why, but I always assumed an epidural was a pill. Perhaps because it's referred to as "an" epidural the same way people refer to "an" Advil. Or, maybe it was subconscious. The word epidural does sound like pill. Epidural, pill. Epidural, pill. Okay, that's a bit of a stretch, I admit.

In reality, an epidural typically refers to liquid anesthetic administered with a syringe (followed by a catheter) into the spine. It's not specific to childbirth, and the name actually derives from the epidural space in the spinal column where the drugs are released.

I remember the day I learned what it really was. It stuck with me because my version was so much milder than the truth. On one hand — a pill. On the other — a large needle in your spine. Now that's a gross misconception if I've ever heard one. To me, it's like using a salt shaker only to realize its pepper. Actually, it's more like using a salt shaker and realizing it's cocaine. Like I said — gross misconception.

SHOCKING FACT #13
PUSHING HAPPENS IN INTERVALS

In movies, when women are in labor, they push, and push, and push. They push hard and they push long. They also scream really loud. As I'm sure you've realized, movies are not encyclopedias. In the pursuit of drama and good ratings, they tend to embellish the truth.

So, what is the truth? Is labor not long? Is it not hard or loud? Of course, it's all of the above. But movies skip over (at least) one thing – namely, the fact that pushing isn't continuous. I had always assumed there were waves of contractions and then a period of pushing. I didn't know the pushing matched the waves of contractions.

Sure, it makes sense to push when contractions hit, but here's the million dollar question: what do you do between pushes? The extreme nature of pushing lends itself to a dramatic climax like the kind you see in movies – not to the repetitive starting and stopping of real life. A round of pushing is roughly one minute of extremely intense, gut wrenching, vein-popping action. Then – nothing. Just three to five minutes of mind-numbing awkward silence or even worse — small talk.

In our birthing suite, there was me, my wife, the nurse, and the doctor. We had been together in the same room for some time – at least enough time to cover all of the good "small talk topics." By the end of it, I'm sure we covered everything from European history to modern robotics. If you haven't packed your hospital bag yet, I suggest including some conversation starters because when a round of pushing ends, the same question is inevitably asked, "So, what were we talking about?" I'm telling you now — bring some cue cards.

SHOCKING FACT #14
IT MAY RIP

When discussing childbirth (I'm sure it's one of your favorite dinner topics), I often hear the same reactions from non-parents. Specifically, when a parent finishes telling the story about their magical, one-of-a-kind birth experience, one of my non-parent friends will say, "I just don't get how something so big can just squeeze through something so small."

In response to this comment, my parent friends will look at each other, and give a dramatic eye roll.

Then, someone will pipe up and say, "It's just one of nature's wonderous miracles."

Twenty-year-old me totally bought this answer. Thirty year-old me calls, "Time out!" Is childbirth amazing? Of course. Is it an incredible act of human strength? Certainly. It is truly a function of incredible design. Props God. Nice work. But there's a lot more to it – the magic act isn't without illusion. Behind the scenes, it's messy. Really messy. The truth is, it doesn't "just squeeze through." Collateral damage is actually very common.

When a woman gives birth to a nine pound baby, it's not clean, and it's not easy. Many women experience a perineal tear in childbirth. Essentially, the tissue between the vagina and rectum can rip. There are varying degrees of tearing, and it can be caused simply from giving birth to a large baby. If you're not squinting or squirming as you read this, something's wrong with you because I'm squirming as I write it.

Let's all just agree now – this sucks. If by chance, you're a misogynist jerk, and you thought women weren't carrying enough of the weight (pun intended), I think this seals the deal. And men – if you needed another reason to feel guilty for just sitting there all comfortable while she endures hell, this is it.

SHOCKING FACT #15
IT MAY NEED TO BE CUT

I f you read the last chapter, you know by now what "it" is. It does all the heavy lifting. It undergoes serious stress. It is quite a powerful little masterpiece – very impressive. On baby day, it performs like a gymnast at the olympics. Men, our "it" isn't nearly as functional as theirs is.

For all that it can do, there are times when it simply can't handle the pressure. Sometimes the request is so great that it simply cannot compute. Error 404 – file not found. As outlined in the last chapter, sometimes it tears. Read "tears" as in ripping, which rhymes with cares. Not "tears" as in crying, which rhymes with fears. Actually, scratch that. Both work. Read it as both.

In an effort to prevent the worst tears, and for a variety of other reasons including the baby's shoulders being stuck, doctors commonly cut the perineal tissue. It's called an episiotomy, and basically, it's when the doctor applies a local anesthetic, and makes a planned, surgical incision on the perineum and the posterior vaginal wall. Usually, it's performed in the second stage of labor, and the incision can be made vertically or diagonally south from the vagina.

Apparently, these are being done less and less often in western countries. I don't know enough about it to know for sure if that's a positive thing (I trust it is), but from my point of view (the view of a nervous dad, sympathetic husband, and innocent bystander in a constant state of shock with all things baby-related), I'll agree with anything that's in the best interest of my wife's baby factory, as long as she and the baby are safe.

I think female genetalia deserves a toast. Wouldn't you agree? Cheers to "it!"

SHOCKING FACT #16
IT'S NOT JUST BABIES WHO POOP

P oop. It's something a parent needs to get used to. Whenever my friends discuss their foray into parenthood, the topic of poop *always* comes up. Changing a dirty diaper has even become a parental right of passage. The adventures of defecation go above and beyond the typical slobber or burp scenario, so I'm sure we can all agree, there's a certain folklore around poop when you have a baby. In a sense, you need to embrace this spirit of adventure, or else become overwhelmed with its frightening arrival.

Generally, if you're having a child, the idea of changing a poopy diaper is accepted. By that time, you've been warned about it by everyone and their grandmother. You've been trained. You've prepared yourself mentally for the vast array of colors, shapes, and sizes that can escape the anus of your child. Not to mention – it happens at unexpected times, in unexpected places, and at unexpected altitudes. However, where baby poop is expected, mother poop is not. When a woman gives birth, poop is involved. Yes, I'm sorry to tell you that poop plays a role even in childbirth.

The muscles that are used to push a child down the birth canal are, apparently, the same muscles that are used to push fecal matter down the rectal canal. I apologize for the graphic nature of this chapter. I realize that simply reading this may cause you to be sick, or even run and hide in the closet to cry in the dark. If you didn't think that blood, guts, and amniotic fluid were enough to behold at that magical moment, I'm less than happy to announce the presence of one more bodily function: the poop. When I learned that women can poop during childbirth, I was stunned. The look on my face said it all, and I assumed that because I had never heard of such a thing, it must be rare. Well, I was wrong. In fact, defecating in labor is not just common, but very common. So ladies, all I can give you is a tip of my hat, and a wish of good luck. And lads, welcome to parenthood. Welcome to poop.

SHOCKING FACT #17
THERE'S MORE COMING

There's a scene in Star Wars where Han Solo is chasing three or four stormtroopers down a corridor of the Death Star. They run through a passageway, and turn a corner where a few dozen more are waiting to attack. Han comes to a halt, and runs away from the group he was just chasing. This scene is the only way I can describe how one might feel at the pinnacle of childbirth. Since I haven't experienced it myself (did I mention I'm a man?), I can't say for sure, but I imagine a woman in labor feels a bit like Han Solo when they realize there's more to deliver than just the baby.

Like Han Solo, a woman delivering a child has great courage as she chases her goal. I can only imagine her incredible sense of relief when the baby enters the world. But unfortunately, it's not the end. After ejecting a child, she must also usher out something called the afterbirth through that same corridor. Afterbirth consists of a few things like amniotic fluid and parts of the umbilical cord, but mainly the placenta. The placenta is essentially the baby's way of connecting with the mother's resources. It's a transfer point for blood, oxygen, and nutrients. The only downside is that it's huge.

In summary, a new mother is not done when the baby comes out. As if that's not bad enough, the afterbirth can be really big – in some cases larger than the baby! It's not very common for an encore presentation to be more epic than the main event! Perhaps the afterbirth is annoyed that the baby gets all the attention, so it tries to bulk up. I just don't know.

I guess it's never over til it's over.

SHOCKING FACT #18
YOU CAN WATCH

This chapter starts with a confession. Since puberty came knocking on my door, I've secretly enjoyed the act of popping a pimple. I don't know why, I just do. I suppose it's the process of cleansing my body that appeals to me. I'd be willing to bet I'm not the only one either. We all feel better after a grooming session, that's for sure. I'd even go so far as to say that a certain curiosity of one's own body is somewhat normal. When my wife and I took a tour of our hospital's birthing ward, I realized this curiosity can be taken to a whole new level.

The hospital staff was walking us through the facility and showcasing its various amenities. As we entered the birthing suite, they were highlighting certain features, and they came to one that made me double take. It wasn't a machine, or some scary, complicated contraption. No – it was a mirror. A mirror on the edge of the bed.

There were approximately ten other people on our tour, so I didn't want to admit to being naive, but I found the guts to ask, "What is that for?" With a straight face, the woman told me, "It's so your wife can see what's going on." She then proceeded to show us the features of the mirror: how it can clip on and clip off, how it's decked out with macro glass, and how it can swivel, as if this whole thing was completely normal.

Now, you have to understand something. I *do* believe birth is a beautiful thing. But it's the *concept* of birth which is beautiful, not the act of it. From what I've heard, using the mirror is pretty common. Many women opt to have it. But may I just raise this question? Isn't it a little gross? Is it not strangely self-indulgent? To me, it seems to be the same urge as popping a pimple, but fifty times worse. I don't mean to offend you if you're a mirror-user, and if you want to see that kind of thing, go for it. I won't try and stop you. But can I just be honest with you guys? Even the thought of it gives me the heebie-jeebies.

SHOCKING FACT #19
IT'S COMPLICATED

Some of the facts in this book are shocking and funny. Some are shocking and gross. This one is shocking and sad.

With longer life expectancy from the accelerated advancement of medical technology and discovery (yes, I can use big words), we often think that having a baby is relatively simple. Well, it's not. Sure, we have innovative tools at our disposal. Sure, we have the accumulated knowledge of all the greatest medical minds to date. But when you add up all of these things, they still don't eliminate problems completely. In many cases they can minimize or even solve problems, but in pregnancy and childbirth, complications can still arise.

Of all the things that can go wrong in pregnancy, having a miscarriage is one of the worst. It's shocking that they still happen, but the truly shocking fact is that they are still very common. Not somewhat common – very common. One out of five pregnancies ends in miscarriage! It's unbelievable!

Yes, many occur so early that the person never knew they were pregnant, but many don't. It's hard to imagine that in this day and age, there isn't a better way to prevent this traumatic event.

SHOCKING FACT #20
THE ENDING IS OBVIOUS

Since we're (regrettably) moving on from the topic of childbirth, we may as well get this fact out of the way now. No big intro, no burying the lead. Here it is: after the disturbing experience of pushing a human being out of their vaginas, women often end up with hemorrhoids.

This book is filled with "that's life." I know that's not grammatically correct, but I'm going with it. It's also filled with "tough luck" and "that's just the way it is." So often, the gruesome details are unexpected and unfortunate, but not this time. Unfortunate, yes. Unexpected, no. Honestly, I saw this one coming. It makes perfect sense. It would be a miracle if you were able to push that hard for that long, and not end up with hemorrhoids. Maybe you haven't followed that road of logic to its obvious conclusion, but once you do, it's pretty clear where it leads. It leads to hemorrhoids.

REFERENCE LIST

Chapter 1 - Morris, Desmond. *Amazing Baby*. Firefly Books Ltd., 2008. (page 32)

Chapter 2 - http://www.babycenter.com/0_sleep-problem-snoring_7541.bc

http://www.whattoexpect.com/pregnancy/symptoms-and-solutions/snoring.aspx

Chapter 3 - Auerbach, Robert D. *Pregnancy Book*. Budlong Press, 2012. (page 86)

Chapter 4 - http://americanpregnancy.org/pregnancy-health/breast-changes-during-pregnancy/

Chapter 5- http://americanpregnancy.org/pregnancy-health/breast-changes-during-pregnancy/

Chapter 6- http://www.webmd.com/baby/features/memory_lapse_it_may_be_pregnancy_brain

Chapter 7- http://www.webmd.com/baby/posture?page=3

http://www.webmd.com/baby/posture?page=4

Chapter 8 - http://www.justthefactsbaby.com/pregnancy/article/third-trimester-infant-development-57

http://www.livestrong.com/article/208955-how-much-weight-does-a-baby-gain-in-the-third-trimester/

Chapter 9 - http://www.webmd.com/baby/inducing-labor-naturally-can-it-be-done

Chapter 10- http://www.webmd.com/baby/guide/vaginal-birth-after-cesarean-vbac-overview

Chapter 11- http://www.whattoexpect.com/pregnancy/
symptoms-and-solutions/water-breaking-during-
pregnancy.aspx

Chapter 12 - http://americanpregnancy.org/labor-and-
birth/epidural/

https://en.wikipedia.org/wiki/Epidural

Chapter 13 - http://www.babies.sutterhealth.org/
laboranddelivery/labor/ld_push.html

Chapter 14- Auerbach, Robert D. *Pregnancy Book*.
Budlong Press, 2012. (page 143)

https://en.wikipedia.org/wiki/Perineal_tear

Chapter 15 - https://en.wikipedia.org/wiki/Episiotomy

Chapter 16 - http://www.whattoexpect.com/pregnancy/
photo-gallery/what-really-happens-during-labor.
aspx#/slide-7

Chapter 17 - https://en.wikipedia.org/wiki/Placental_
expulsion

Chapter 18 - http://transitionsbirthclass.com/
wordpress/the-mirror/

Chapter 19- Auerbach, Robert D. *Pregnancy Book*.
Budlong Press, 2012. (page 35)

https://en.wikipedia.org/wiki/Miscarriage

Chapter 20- http://baby.about.com/od/parents5/p/

Hemorrhoids-After-Birth.htm

SPECIAL THANKS

This book wouldn't have been possible without the support of the following people:

-Mike & Colleen Dugan

-Melody Welton

-Justin & Shawnna Gunnink

-Benjamin & Maryann Roebuck

-Steve & Cindy Best

-Don & Donna Vander Linde

-Jason & Laura Glerum

-Caleb & Alex Groeneweg

-Jenn & Ben Meador

Additional thanks to Kyle & Katie Bultman for photography, and to all models in the book.

ABOUT THE AUTHOR

This is Joshua Best's first book. He wrote it in the Notes App on his iPhone 4S. It was written with one hand, while bouncing a screaming baby to sleep with the other. If you think that's an easy feat, you give it a try.

Originally from Ontario, Canada, he currently lives in Grand Rapids, Michigan with his wife and two children. He is not qualified to write a book about babies in the least. He works in advertising for crying out loud! In fact, Joshua Best has only one relevant credential: Dad.

His wife, April Best, edited this book, and would like to note that if it wasn't for her, this whole thing wouldn't be possible. For reals, yo.

W! OH THE HUM
HY OH WHY? SERENITY NOW!
WHIZ! SHOOT DARN IT! WHAT THE?!? HE
ODNESS! WHAT IS THAT? GASP! AHHH! G
THERE'S NO WAY! OH MY GOODNESS! W
NITY NOW! OH THE HUMANITY! SERIOUS
WHAT THE?!? HEY! WHY OH WHY? SE
GEE WHIZ! SHOOT DARN IT! WHAT THE
OH MY GOODNESS! WHAT IS THAT? GASP
ANITY! SERIOUSLY??? THERE'S NO WAY
WHY OH WHY? SERENITY NOW! OH THE
GEE WHIZ! SHOOT DARN IT! WHAT THE?
HAT IS THAT? SERIOUSLY??? GASP! AHH
THERE'S NO WAY! OH MY GOODNES
ITY! SERENITY NOW! OH THE
THE?!? HEY